Essential Question
What can our connections to the world teach us?

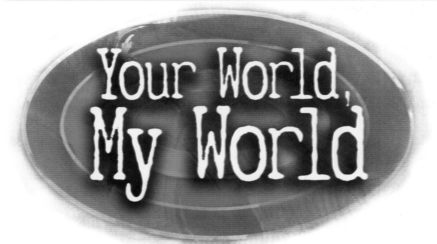

by **Marie Langley**
illustrated by **Nina de Polonia**

CHAPTER 1

Summer Camp Connection

"So that's your bus over there, and this is mine," Emilia said, dropping her bags on the ground as she turned to give Crystal a hug. "It's been so much fun, hasn't it?"

"It's been amazing!" Crystal replied. "I can't believe I didn't even want to come to summer camp. I'm so glad Mom talked me into it."

"So am I," said Emilia. "If you hadn't come to camp, we wouldn't be friends."

All around, the air was thick with voices and laughter as other campers said their good-byes. Luggage was being stowed, and under the watchful eyes of the camp counselors, passengers began to fill the buses. At last, the bus engines chugged to life.

"I'd better get on," Emilia said, moving away.

"You'll e-mail, won't you, Em?" Crystal called after her.

"Of course. And I'll call you. We'll see each other again soon!" With a final wave, Emilia disappeared onto the bus.

Crystal waved back, then gathered up her mandolin case and backpack and ran to board her bus home.

As the long journey homeward began, Crystal leaned against the bus window, staring out but only vaguely seeing the landscape roll by. She was busy rewinding events in her mind, searching for the moment when her friendship with Emilia began.

When Crystal had arrived at summer camp, all she'd wanted to do was go home. She was sure that Mom was wrong, and that camp was going to be a total disaster. Crystal had kept her head down. Her curtain of blond hair helped her avoid eye contact when she was shown to the cabin she'd be sharing with other girls. She had barely had time to dump her gear on her bed when she was startled by a loud, cheerful voice right in her ear.

"No way! You've got a mandolin? That is so cool! Mind if I take a look?" Another girl was standing next to Crystal and smiling as she reached toward the mandolin case. Crystal responded with a half-smile and a small nod of her head. The other girl opened the case and lifted out the mandolin.

Because of the careful way this girl with dark, friendly eyes and even darker curly hair handled the mandolin, Crystal immediately warmed to her.

"Do you play?" Crystal asked.

"Yeah, I guess, but … I'm not that good. I'm Emilia, by the way. What's your name?"

"I'm Crystal. Do you have a mandolin?"

"I get to play Poppa's—my grandfather's. He plays really well, and he's taught me a few songs. You're so lucky to have this here!"

So the connection was made, and the conversation moved along easily. Crystal discovered that Emilia lived with her parents in New York City.

"Lots of my family is there," Emilia explained. "They immigrated from Italy just before I was born."

"I'm from Roanoke," Crystal explained in exchange. "My family has lived in Virginia for over 100 years."

For years, Emilia had been spending at least part of her summer at camp, and she was more than happy to help Crystal settle in.

Over the following days and weeks, they enjoyed swimming, canoeing, and all the other activities offered at the camp. They also found time to teach each other new melodies on Crystal's mandolin. That was how the friendship deepened.

Once camp was over, it wasn't surprising that the two girls kept in touch. They traded e-mails several times a week. They shared and compared the details of Emilia's life in New York City and Crystal's in Roanoke, Virginia.

Then, halfway through September, Emilia was delighted to receive a phone call. It was Crystal, and she wasn't calling simply to say hello.

"I've asked my mom," Crystal said, "and she says it's fine if I invite you to Roanoke for a weekend in October. What do you think?"

"Really? Oh, wow, I'm so excited!" squealed Emilia. "I'll have to ask my parents, but I'm sure I'll be allowed to visit. I can't wait to see you again!"

"And I can't wait to show you around. We'll have such a great time, you'll see."

STOP AND CHECK

Where is Emilia going? Why?

CHAPTER 2

A Visit to Virginia

"Weren't you scared, flying here by yourself?" Crystal asked. It was Friday afternoon, and Crystal and her mom had just picked up Emilia from Roanoke's airport.

Emilia shrugged. "It was no problem," she said. "I've flown a few times before with my family."

Crystal hadn't flown anywhere. She wasn't sure she could ever be so calm about what Emilia had just done. Crystal glanced over at her mom, who was driving. The brief sympathetic smile she got back said that her mom knew how nervous Crystal would feel about such a trip.

Emilia was gazing out the car window. "It's so great to be here. Look at those trees. The fall colors are amazing!"

"Wait until we go hiking tomorrow," Crystal's mom said. "Then you'll see real color. Crystal is looking forward to showing you her backyard."

Crystal grinned at Mom, happy to be brought back to familiar territory. "You'll love it," she told Emilia. "I hope you brought hiking shoes?"

"I did, but that's thanks to summer camp," Emilia said, smiling. "There's not much need for hiking shoes in New York!"

Crystal's "backyard," as her mom put it, was the Blue Ridge Mountains, not far beyond Roanoke. On Saturday morning, Crystal, Crystal's mom, and Emilia drove to the start of the trail Crystal had chosen.

The trail climbed steadily, and the rich gold, crimson, and yellow colors of fall were everywhere. Crystal named the different tree species. She felt excited showing her friend the familiar trail and enjoyed telling her about the geography and history of the Blue Ridge area.

"Fantastic!" Emilia exclaimed as they admired the view. "This is all really new to me. I love it! But tell me something—are there bears around here?"

"Well, sometimes …" Crystal said. When she saw the sudden look of horror on Emilia's face, she quickly reassured her. "But don't worry, there hasn't been a bear sighting around here for ages, and anyway, we're making so much noise they'd be scared off before we even saw them."

"That's good to know," said Emilia with a relieved smile.

That evening, Emilia joined Crystal and her family for a meal of traditional Appalachian food: chicken and dumplings, green beans, pumpkin, beets, and corn bread.

When everyone had finished the dessert of apple cobbler, Emilia said, "Wow, that meal was amazing!"

But the best was yet to come. After the table was cleared and the dishes done, the family brought out musical instruments. Crystal's father had a banjo, while her mother played the accordion. Crystal's brother brought out his guitar, and Crystal, of course, had her mandolin.

For the next hour or more, Emilia found herself immersed in Appalachian bluegrass music. The instruments sang happily, filling the room with vibrant melodies. Emilia laughed and smiled and clapped until her face and hands hurt. Then Crystal passed her the mandolin.

"Your turn now, Em," Crystal said. "Play one of those Italian tunes your poppa taught you."

"Oh, but I don't play that well ..." Emilia said, but they wouldn't let her refuse. Nervously she began to play one of her poppa's tunes, and the mandolin came to life in her hands. To her delight, the others soon picked up the melody and joined in.

It was pure magic!

Sunday was the last day of Emilia's visit. "I want to show you one more special place," Crystal told her. "It's a place where I help out sometimes."

"Okay," said Emilia. "Surprise me."

Crystal did surprise her. Crystal's mom took Crystal and Emilia to the Roanoke Wildlife Rescue Center.

"This is a place that cares for orphaned or injured wild mammals," said Crystal. "But don't worry—no bears. It's mainly animals like raccoons, groundhogs, and possums. Oh, and sometimes skunks."

Crystal showed Emilia around, introducing her to other volunteers and explaining how the animals were cared for until it was time to return them to the wild.

When it was time to return to New York, Emilia told Crystal about the strongest impressions from her Roanoke visit. "The music was so amazing. I can't wait to tell Poppa! And I learned a ton about wildlife and the environment. Thank you!"

Welcome to the
Wildlife Rescue Center

STOP AND CHECK

What did Emilia learn about music on her visit to Roanoke?

CHAPTER 3

New Directions

Back in New York, Emilia returned to her normal daily routines: home, school, and visiting her poppa at his restaurant in the Little Italy neighborhood in Manhattan. She was happy to be home, but whenever she went out to run an errand in the city, she couldn't help seeing everything a little differently.

New York was a big city, so different from Crystal's home near the Blue Ridge Mountains. And Emilia kept remembering how much Crystal cared about the natural environment and the wildlife where she lived.

She talked to her poppa about it. She'd been trying to show him one of the bluegrass tunes that Crystal played on the mandolin. Emilia couldn't quite get it right, but she knew her poppa understood how much she'd enjoyed sharing the music. Maybe he would also understand about how much Crystal cared for the world around her home.

"Perhaps I should care more, too," Emilia said. "I mean, just because I live in a city doesn't mean there's no natural environment or wildlife, does it, Poppa? Shouldn't we look after those things here as well?"

Her poppa nodded. "It's a big, wide world," he said. "We should all help care for the environment wherever we are."

Emilia sent an e-mail to Crystal describing her conversation with her grandfather. "So I'm going to start actually doing something to show I care," Emilia wrote. "I just have to figure out where to begin."

She knew her school was part of the New York Green Schools program, so she decided to learn more about what that meant.

She discovered that the program was all about waste reduction—reducing, reusing, and recycling. There was a challenge to see which school could come up with the best waste management system, and Emilia volunteered to help.

"We're building bins for food waste and anything else around school that would make good compost," she wrote in her next e-mail to Crystal. "It feels great to be doing something like this. See how you've inspired me!"

The next e-mail Emilia sent Crystal was an invitation. "It's time for you to visit me now," the e-mail said. "Please come to New York!"

Crystal loved the idea of seeing Emilia again, spending time hanging out, and maybe even playing music. At the same time, she was terrified.

Attending summer camp had been her first big trip away from home on her own. Emilia had turned that into a great experience, but could Emilia get a small-town girl to relax and enjoy gigantic New York City?

Crystal told her mom she didn't want to go.

"Don't say no right away," said her mom. "Give yourself some time to think about it."

Crystal went up to her room. She picked up the mandolin and began to practice a melody that Emilia had taught her. There were some parts that she couldn't quite remember, and Emilia wasn't there to help her get it right.

"There's so much more I want to learn," Crystal thought. "And it's not just about that tune either, or about the mandolin."

She kept thinking and realized she wanted to learn more about music in general, and about the environment, and about, well … about the whole world! Getting to know Emilia had made her see just how much she still didn't know.

There was a knock on the door, and her mom came in. She sat down beside Crystal on the bed for a moment before speaking.

"When you didn't want to go to summer camp, I was worried," her mom said. "I knew it was important for you to try something away from home on your own. I wanted you to realize that you could stand on your own two feet. Summer camp was the first step, and now Emilia's offered you the chance to take another, bigger step. Do you think you're ready for that?"

Crystal plucked a string on the mandolin, listening to the sound before she replied.

"You know how worried Emilia was about bears on the hike?" Her mom nodded, and Crystal kept talking. "Bears can be scary, but Emilia didn't really need to be scared. Maybe I helped her understand that."

"I'm sure you did," said her mom.

"Well, if I go to New York, she's going to have to help me not be scared every time a siren blares or people bump into me on the sidewalk, and she'll have to help me not get lost, and—"

"I'm sure Emilia will do all that," her mom said.

"Well then, I'd better e-mail Emilia to say I'm coming to New York," said Crystal. Her mom gave her a big hug.

Emilia's reply came back in a flash, full of things they could do in New York and ending with, "If you want, Poppa will teach us some Italian mandolin tunes."

"I can't wait!" Crystal replied.

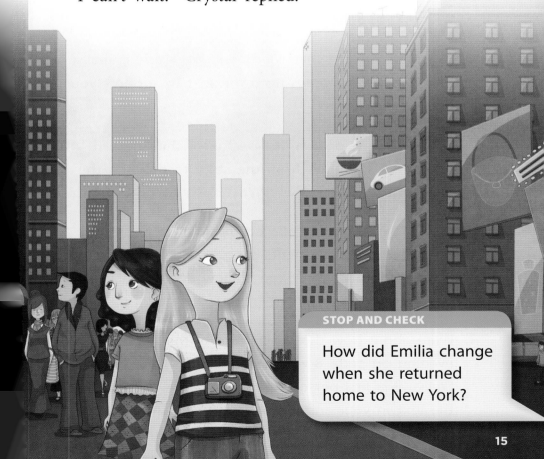

STOP AND CHECK

How did Emilia change when she returned home to New York?

Respond to Reading

Summarize

Use important details from *Your World, My World* to summarize the story. Your graphic organizer may help you.

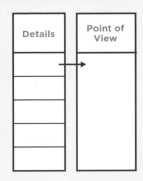

Details	Point of View

Text Evidence

1. How can you tell that *Your World, My World* is realistic fiction? Give examples from the text to support your answer. **GENRE**

2. Is this story told by a first-person or third-person narrator? Use details from the story to describe the narrator's point of view. **POINT OF VIEW**

3. When Crystal's family played music after dinner on page 8, their "instruments sang." Find another example of personification on page 8. How does each example add to the story? **PERSONIFICATION**

4. Write about how the description of the family's evening on page 8 would change if it were written by Emilia as a first-person narrator. Include details from the text in your answer. **WRITE ABOUT READING**

Compare Texts

Read a poem that compares two different ways of life.

Do I Know You?

"I'm a country boy—this photo
  shows where I live.

See how the trees stand up, crowding the
  mountainous ridge?

I'm part of all that, and that's part of me.

When I play you my fiddle, then maybe
  you'll see.

I can play up a storm with lightning
  and thunder,

And each time I do, I can't help but wonder

If my granddaddy never taught me
  the fiddle and banjo too,

Would I hear this land's music
  the way that I do?"

"You say you're from the country
—well, I'm from the city,

And what I see from my window
isn't nearly as pretty

As your mountains and trees,
but I think it's fine.

I love the city—it's home,
and it's mine.

Your granddaddy taught you music?
Well, mine did, too.

I've got his violin—I can show it
to you.

Even better, I'll play tunes that my
poppa taught me,

Folk music from Europe, then
maybe you'll see

How family and home are part of me, too,

And it's always a mix of the old and the new.

Yes, I love this city—it's home, and it's mine,

But I'm happy to share it with you any time!"

Make Connections

How do the two speakers in *Do I Know You?* make connections with different parts of the world?
ESSENTIAL QUESTION

Compare the two characters in *Your World, My World* with the two speakers in *Do I Know You?* How are they alike? **TEXT TO TEXT**

Focus on Literary Elements

Imagery Poets and other writers use imagery to give readers a stronger sense of the ideas they are writing about. Imagery can include the use of metaphor and simile, or it can simply use vivid descriptive words. Imagery often uses the senses (touch, sight, hearing, smell, and taste) to help readers form mental images of what it is the writer is describing.

Read and Find In *Do I Know You?* the descriptions in the first verse (page 17) help us visualize the country boy's life. He describes how he "can play up a storm," and the metaphor helps us form an image in our minds of how the music could sound. In the next verse, the words help us visualize the city with its "mix of the old and the new" (page 19).

Your Turn

Close your eyes and remember a scene from your early childhood. It could be meeting a relative, attending a special event, or visiting a new place. Imagine this with all your senses. What can you see, hear, smell, taste, and feel? Then write words or phrases that show what you saw, heard, smelled, tasted, and touched. Use these notes to help you draw a picture of the scene you imagined. Label the picture with the words you wrote.